BLOOD MEMORY

Pitt Poetry Series
Ed Ochester, Editor

BLOOD MEMORY

COLLEEN J. MCELROY

University of Pittsburgh Press

Published by the University of Pittsburgh Press, Pittsburgh, Pa., 15260
Copyright © 2016, Colleen J. McElroy
All rights reserved
Manufactured in the United States of America
Printed on acid-free paper
10 9 8 7 6 5 4 3 2 1
ISBN 13: 978-0-8229-6408-7
ISBN 10: 0-8229-6408-2

for my mother Ruth Celeste Johnson
(1911–2012)
a wreath of memories

Memories of the outside world will never have the same tonality as those of home and, by recalling these memories, we add to our store of dreams; we are never real historians, but always near poets, and our emotion is perhaps nothing but an expression of a poetry that was lost.

—**Gaston Bachelard**

What I like about photographs is that they capture a moment that is gone forever, impossible to reproduce.

—**Karl Lagerfeld**

Culture is the process by which a person becomes all that they were created capable of being.

—**Thomas Carlyle**

CONTENTS

I

II

BLOOD MEMORY

The Family Album

call it blood memory for I am the only
one left to identify by name the ancestors

I am the only one left of the women
who sat around grandmother's oak table
and wove the stories of who and where
who knows the half of it and when

I am the answer to the question
my mother's sisters swallowed:
What will you do with that child?

I know now that I am here to give
voice to tongues never silent
and doors closing too quickly

I am of the age where death comes
easily and visits often in those little
obit notes of passing reminding us

how we've neglected dear ones
now lived again through fading pictures
stuck to crumbling pages

I buy tickets to places I may never visit
spend hours trying to remember
if the image stuck in my head has origins

in a dream or some foggy night
slipping past almost unnoticed

I am the last female of a family
of women who wove the fabric
of stories into doilies and slip covers

I am the child with sparrow legs
sock heels stuck halfway in her shoes
drinking the last of metaphors left
in teacups on the table unattended

Les Anciens

circa 1870s

Anna Belle was not the prettiest Perry Lee said
yet under the scars of those awful plantation years
she was the softest with a shy smile *little bitty thing*
just a handful he said to the memory of watching
her walk in the shadows between cabins
where to be a slave death had walked so easily

he took this sandy colored woman for his wife
took her sister Ethel and brother Roman too
northbound with his twin and their risky business
of horses at a time when colored folk
never owned so much as their names
and Perry Lee's father, a freedman
with oaken skin worked iron and horse
shoes and taught his sons how to soothe

skittery colts by looking them in the eyes
taught Perry to pretend not to read
when reading could get a colored man
hanged—taught them to fend for themselves
they had been heading west from the river delta
through the deep South when Perry saw Anna Belle
the first time he looked into her eyes
he could almost see the drowning pool
where slave women took babies
rather than have them sold at auction

Anna Belle was just old enough to be trusted
to do the cookhouse chores when Emancipation came
no one knew she'd live nearly one hundred years
a century to hold onto the shadow of those days
slow to fade yet seen those long months ahead
whenever she turned away—Perry Lee took her
north and when they crossed the Natchez River
she looked back only once as Perry Lee held her

they followed the underground escape route
until they reached that crook in the Mississippi
there he cradled her in the steamboat's bow and
later when they settled on earned land my grandfather
bought a shelf of leather bound books and a roll top desk
my grandmother brought the old ways cooking from scratch
his push against her pull like they had all the time in the world

A Sounding in the Woods

the way the family told it Papa's brother Jackson was the trouble maker—said
he turned bad after their daddy was kidnapped by Johnny Reb—*conscripted*
they said but everyone knew he was taken in the war between the North and
South because he had a way with saddles and rigs—because he could shoe
a coltish horse and set it loose before the nails cooled down—everybody
knew Johnny Reb needed a man like that free or slave to keep the horses
halfway fit—knew they didn't care that taking him meant leaving behind two
scraggly colored boys and a woman hid away somewhere—said they came
looking for him in broad daylight the story goes—came galloping through
the brush until the dry leaves rustled like a crackling fire and the hounds
itched to be let loose—a sounding in the woods that told them something
was wrong—and even long after the war Jackson would bolt at the least bit
of movement in the inconvenient light on a dark road that led them out of
town—Papa went north Jackson went west leaving behind the one thing that
told it all—when I found the long bullet in the middle drawer under Papa's
shaving bowl he told me it was the one that misfired when Jackson pulled
him out of the river—said it creased Jackson's hat and his too—said he kept
it for good luck the way some folks kept a rabbit's foot—said *by rights this
belongs to Jackson*—I turned the shell over in my hand—all that copper light
like a bright button—I wondered if Jackson had another with him on days he
rode the rodeo days he found himself cornered in South Dakota or his face
on a poster in Wyoming—Papa said they never thought to load the bullet
even when white folks paid them a few coins or corn meal mush and clabber
milk for a job that took all day—told me that bullet was the one thing they
owned outright—and even later even after I learned about firing pins and
gun powder learned a bullet was a blind thing that knew no man I'd look at
it and wonder what luck it held to keep Papa safe a while longer

Badlands

1.

the story goes soon as Perry Lee and Jackson
settled Anna Belle and her family
on a spit of a farm in Illinois they set out
to look for their sister Dora Emma
they followed the underground route
leading them due west and steered clear
of towns where faces held the pallor of hunger
that marked the southern states   towns where
you move around and turn around and jump just so
while carpet baggers carried a gun in one pocket
and the law in the other ready to shoot or shackle
what they called runaway negras
the posters were everywhere
as Perry and Jackson dark as rain-soaked tree bark
rode with the sun behind them

2.

word came their ma'am was living with her folks
out there on the endless plains   a map fitting Jackson's
need to head for the badlands soon as he could
Jackson rode easy at night using stars to navigate
the way the old folks had done to escape paddyrollers
Perry Lee took the reins of the buckboard brought along
to ease the travel for their ma'am and their baby sister
Dora Emma not old enough to gentle a horse at night
when the moon's borrowed light tricked both horse and man
or by day when the prairie sun bleached the land to sand
and tumbleweed ten hands high spooked the horses
tilting the weight of the buckboard
until Jackson tied bags of loose dirt to opposite rails

3.

miles on the other side of the Indian mounds
they skirted towns that looked suspicious
circling to keep close to any wooded space
a shadow ahead of ex–slave catchers
itching to return to their trade
twice a wheel broke and they had to make
a soldering fire for the spokes hoping
they could remember what their Pap had taught them
they were looking for a colored settlement
somewhere near a stream or a ridge blocking
winds that carved their due on everything
the way their mother's people braved winter
they looked for houses hunkered together
near but away from the edges of a town

4.

story goes they knocked on doors where they saw
a colored woman hanging the wash
sheets meant there was a place to rest
overalls meant men would soon come looking
they figured their ma'am and sister made the trek
late summer when she got no word after their father
disappeared and all those migrating north had set
the two of them running   following the old trails
as far as they could even though the signs
that made escape easier years ago had been scrambled
after the war and that talk about forty acres and a mule
about who owned the land and who was working it for free

5.

Jackson and Perry Lee rode through flatlands
where hills and burial mounds etched the sky

wood sparrows darted among canopies of cottonwoods
meadow flowers flamed colors in the tall grass

coyotes kept their distance and the wind never let up
they were stopped at the Kansas border

because they resembled a negro man on a wanted poster
some old gun-slinger like Isom Dart

or worse some lawman sure their features spoke
of Indian roots: the eagle-like nose and dark eyes

watching silent as the lawman seemed ready to prove
to the town he'd have none of the likes of them

the sight of their six foot frames made folks look away
even homesteaders wanted them to move on quickly

6.

Jackson cut his brother's hair and tied back his own
to smudge the familiar Indian-ness at first glance
they ran out of underground markers ran out of safe
houses that would send them to the next town

where post riders or the telegraph passed through
still the air was clear of sudden fires and gun powder smells
lingering those long years after the war in southern fields
they were out in open country when they found the sod house

empty despite the covered well and twig broom by the door
the place looked lost as if no soul had ever wandered there
a rabbit disappeared like quicksilver through a hole
and white butterflies swirled around the grinding stone

in one corner a grain basket slumped of its own weight
they looked for signs to say how recent ma'am had been there
truth was their mother's people had to keep moving
same as anyone wandering that side of the Mason-Dixon

7.

when Perry Lee's horse went lame he stayed behind
while Jackson moved on toward Okfuskee
the story goes that Jackson changed horses twice
culled a new steed from a moving pack of wild ones
a habit he did not break until age caught up with him
until one sheriff too many sent him running west again
a new moon had come and gone before he returned
by that time Perry Lee had readied the house for their ma'am
stacked wood by a south wall to keep winds at bay
all for nothing when Jackson came back with Dora Emma
alone sitting tall in the saddle more man than woman
sunburnt in Indian garb the Creek way beads braided in her hair

8.

she told them how their ma'am died chopping wood
when the axe slipped and no one there to stop the bleeding
said their mother's people took her in for the time being

said the time ran out when Jackson showed up
they waited until the wind stopped howling like a hungry wolf
and spring crept onto the prairie in clumps of yellow buds

Perry wanted Jackson to come home with him and Dora
to be a family that wouldn't have to go looking for each other
until he saw how Jackson was bent on striking out on his own

where Jackson said man horse and rabbit all had the same
chances and nobody asking them to jump Jim Crow
said he had to git to gittin' Civil War or no

at night Dora Emma slept between the two
a sound dreamless sleep that gave her comfort

9.

they sat out before dawn when the sky was pink
and they could ride into the sun until the foothills
the river was not yet swollen with spring rains
streaks of silver fish darted just below the surface
bottom fish stirred mud which gave the river its name
they had safely reached the river once again both of them
Perry the one who would be my grandfather
and Jackson the other my mother insisted all her life
remained a horse thief long after he stopped riding
the chaparral and came to die in Los Angeles of old age
Jackson stayed with them as far as the steamboat landing
loaded Dora Emma first to the deck where colored
were cradled next to cargo where both air and food carried
gritty traces of cinders and oil and the sweat of roustabouts
Jackson steadied his horse until there was nothing to see
but gray water churning where jack salmon dived for cover

Jackson

papa's twin kept
his distance   until

                                                        distance kept him
                          long after
the west tamed   other men
                          Jackson stayed
somewhere   between
the hole-in-the-wall   and paradise
folks   back home
                          talked   nothing else
even when   word came
he stole horses   seeing as how
                                                        Reconstruction
made horse   thieving   unnecessary
                                                        and all of us
waiting to see   his mug
                          at the post office

                                                        riding Isom Dart
a price on his
head more than   he was worth
                          posted by the door
                                                        some glass plate
photo   a sepia blur   stamping him
wanted   leaving him
                                                        sidestepping
                          just before   the sheriff
came looking   for black outlaws
                          under every bush
leaving him   hiding Brer
                          Rabbit scared
                          Jackson
the family's   pride   and a crying shame
                          Papa's double
tall and lanky   a regular cowboy
                          wild as the horses
he stole   still   folks said
                          hustling
was in his blood   even with that house
off Hollywood hills   where in those days
                          anything was
                          possible

The Hanged Man

when the hanged man shits
we know death has taken over
the drool on his lips harden
where the tongue gargoyles out and
his eyes squeeze on a bit of last light
more often than not his genitals stiffen
then hang tumescent as if they
like him have lost directions
the rancid breath rales clicking
like vultures feeding or something
hissing toward candle flame
only the dead can see while
legs dance joyously to a melody
only the hanged man hears
feet pointed as if to pirouette
while hooded figures job done
disappear in the copse of trees and black
faces look up into the even blacker
night full of screams fading into the wind
like the hooting of owls or bull frogs
croaking in muddy shallows
throats expanding contracting
the story passed on and consumed
in a single photo in a family album
an uncle a cousin or brother
Ethel's boy or Roman's eldest
dragged from his bed by men
in shiny boots and white hoods
and slung from the boughs of a tree
a grainy reminder of what
grief we have never digested
and the tree itself still twisted
and misshapen a century later
as if despite the southern sun
fire still burns brightly at its roots

Gandy Dancer

Son was a high yella man
skin the color of russet potatoes
eyes the color of agates or cats
even women whistled when he passed
so pretty he could have been a changeling
"Indian from them high cheek bones,"
the old women laughed—"and them eyes"
they said "them eyes could charm
the stink out of a skunk"—so naturally
the women in the family tried
to hide him from the world
and its 1930s rage and hunger
but he busted loose—broke out
stayed so long that when he returned
the family hardly knew him
"as I live and breathe" they said
looking at his white Panama hat
two toned shoes and empty pockets
he just wasn't the same when he came
back from the Zone—all pins and needles
said he lost the way things smelled
his senses plugged with odors of death and dirt
where the bossman said the canal was to be
and his mother wailing nearly every hour
the handsomest of all her boys downcast
instead of staring holes through any woman
and Son washing himself in Fels Naptha
slicking pomade in his hair with little finger waves
his good clothes in a paperboard suitcase
the note to his mama on the kitchen table

Roman

he died on a white hot day in August
his mouth full of strange silence
Mama said it was hard to tell
when a colored man was crazy
or just fed up with white folks
said we had to remember what happened
to Uncle Roman's wife, Clara, and his son
Mama said everyone knew what was eating him
what he had seen when he helped
Papa move all the families to Missouri
towns burnt black in smoldering hatred
some said Roman saw a line of colored women
hanging from a bridge   skirts fluttering
one woman eight months gone   swaying
her belly so big the weight pulled
the rope around her neck even tighter
no one remembers when he began
to take too much comfort in a child's
laughter or when he heard a mother whisper
"get Roman away from that baby"
after that he began to stay home all day
coming out in the shelter of night
when he watched the river slide under
the shadows of the long railroad Bridge
no one knew what Roman saw those nights
and after he died the old women
clicked their tongues and shook their heads
in the gone-too-soon of it all

For the Want of a Shoe

everyone said Dora Emma was mannish
not so much the way she dressed
buying fancy whenever she had the money

buying special made when she had gold
buying shoes with shiny buckles to hide
the calluses on her feet: *clodhoppers, honey*

leave ruts in the road some said
wasn't so much the way she dressed
but how she set about working

hauling as much as any man
half grown her size and refusing
to sweep and clean the great houses

up river on the other side
even when the money was better
and she had a chance to find a man

come courting on his day off
Dora Emma's mannerisms showed
she wasn't waiting for some man

even back then when there was no name
for Dora Emma and her brazen women friends
no one could say what they were doing up in there

most thought Dora hinkty and plain some-timey
refusing help when needed and sporting
riding breeches when decent women were fanning

away the heat under a shade tree
they should have asked Dora Emma
why she was the way she was

she would have told them
how much she remembered
back when she had no ma or pa

back when living depended on how far
she could run bare foot
on an empty stomach to bring water

so everybody bathed but her and how
her hair was raked until her scalp hurt
she could have told them

her Indian name or how to find
soft shell crabs in the tide pools
instead she built the finest house

in the valley and entertained
endless games of faro for a few coins
and a certain amount of laughter

Rebel

1928 and Papa's sister Dora Emma
bought a Model T then headed
down Highway 67 Chicago bound alone
picture that: a colored woman
sitting tall in one of Henry's finest
big white southern hat perched
on freshly pressed curls
Gibson blouse crisp as snow
everything about her shiny brand new
some said she got the cash
from the proceeds of her house
of ill repute [*shame* they clucked]
others said her brother coughed up money
bootlegging beer from the Griesedieck boys
not that it mattered taking from gangsters
folks said no amount of velvet and lace
could hide what Dora had been those years
before she got it in her head to do better
said she had nerve going through
Cairo [said to rhyme with Karo]
after all that mess that caused families
to get out of Illinois burning behind them
those that kept track saw her shifting
on the upgrades high in the seat
like she was still on a buckboard
the ribbons on her hat dancing
in the wake of her passing
the note on the seat beside her reading
"You are missed. Everybody says Hi"

Ablution

when the tools are laid out
stainless steel gleams like mirrors
speculum, catheter, scalpel sharp
handles smooth as kid leather
she climbs onto the saddle
of the table—her feet slip into
metal stirrups—the doctor's standard
poodle nuzzles her arm
then goes to his blanket in the corner
by the fireplace—she thinks
how lucky for a colored girl to find
a room so clean—she imagines
the dog twitching his nose
as he watches her brown legs
spread eagle under the white cloth
his coat shiny as a new tuxedo
she hears him lapping water
a sound she carries with her
as the doctor lays the rubber gloves
on her belly and washes her clean
she makes the least suspenseful
movement—turns her head to look
at the back door bolted shut
now that she has entered—the dog
laps more water—a sound she remembers
when her mother announces she has waited
supper until her daughter returned
her sisters pry with coded questions
but she is good at keeping secrets
never telling the boy's name
or where he had taken her
she hears only that lonely
sound of the dog lapping water
a single movement so brief
she has to bend toward her plate
slumping forward—not hearing her father
push away from the table—sending water
glasses spilling—forks rattling
against knives—staining the bone
white table cloth—the rush of blood
that flows from her like a river

as she becomes the one we never speak
about—defiant beautiful fierce—Fanny
one photo frozen for the long goodbye

Sepia Women

in the '30s when my mother's sister
worked for the mortician leaving
the family fit to be tied
Jennie said she never even thought
about the folks she worked on being dead
until Claudia cooked up a fuss and said
the cancer she got later came
from the chemicals for dead folks
Jennie said I'm a grown ass woman
doing what I want to do
Lord knows even folks like us need
a pinch of color from time to time—
Papa said she was too pretty
to be working on dead people
wasn't no kin to her
Jennie said they were just clients
same as the beauty shop offered
except they were laid out
on a satin bed and never asked
for a mirror to check her work—
stuffing the cheeks with cotton
on a crochet hook was her specialty
she said they all looked so fragile
faces frozen in old time daguerreotypes
where the light was fading fast
and a quiet crept into the frame—
one day she up and quit the mortuary
when her father called to see
just what she did in all that dim light—
the photography studio was right
next door so she took her skills there
tinting grainy sepia to flush
sallow cheeks and feathered lips
before they bled into the background
bringing them out of the shadows
until they stood in all their glory

A Given Name

Colleen-a Stringbean-a Stick Stack Stina

my birth father's name was a song
all by itself: Purcia Purcell
like pearls falling from a necklace
a shadowy figure my mother ignored
escaping like the nomad on the tapestry
in the living room the one room no one entered
my mother's second husband
came marching in with a name
double clicked with military precision
Jesse Dalton—here's J.D. hut-two-three
the cadence of my birth father's song forever dimmed
my grandfather's mother died with an Indian name
whispered only by a few
their footprints erased by prairie winds
my grandmother went always
by the name Mama not Belle or Anna
and never mentioned her mother's name
lost in the storms of southern rebellion
I called my mother Ruth until high school
where my friends used Ma, Moms, Mama
and I learned to conform
my cousin's name was Modestine
her sleep filled with immodest dreams
but she riled stubborn if ever someone asked:
where did you get that name?
same place you got yours: she'd snarl
and stare them down until they turned away
I was born on the same day
in the same hospital as my cousin
Loveta *down the hall:* my mother said
I wondered if Loveta's mother
said: *up the hall* if she ever thought
of me and her baby in the same nursery
I wondered if we sensed
in our separate bassinets
family near by yet far away
I wondered if Loveta found love
followed her name and if she ever
answered: *all names are made up*
to those who questioned the origins

of such delicious belongings on colored children
my family was fraught with Mae's
and Belles and Jeans sung with a twist
Jennie Mae brought me turpentine
to remove my boyfriend's three part
name written in wall paint on the toilet
of the two Jeans, Cora was the baby
until Irma came home with a baby
nestled in the crook of her arm
as if a child had always been there
Charzelle and Mercedees
my cousins removed once or twice
in beautiful treble their names
the names that we alone own
the names we hope would carry us past
a snag in the road, past the poison
of a single dark lens, past dogs
and fire hoses and the riots of now
the names that call us home

—*for Marisis, Remica, Lou Oma, Senesta, Makaleia, Chakema, Eustacia, and all those of wonderful names*

All That They Were

in the photo album Papa's daughters
sport a century of profiles they inherited
fighting the world they fight themselves

in each photo my mother the darkest one sits apart
turned slightly to stare into some vague distance
fighting the world she fights herself

each of her sisters defy the lens
pointed at them their eyes blazing
to fight the world they fought themselves

my mother the slender one fought her sisters'
sermons of wide hips streaked with color stoked barbs
snip-snip of the world they fought to fight themselves

her skin dark as the inside rim of a walnut shell
my mother the fledgling tasted the razor's edge of words
her sisters taught to rope the world they battled in themselves

she the last girl caught between the only son and
a long line of yella women salting the tongue
fought the world alone and kept it to herself

though she never controlled the world like the others
she laid them all to rest changing the story to suit her best
still fighting the world she fought herself

they were none of them all bad nor good these women
sisters of my mother who could never speak true
the story of this world they found fighting themselves

Lawdy Miz Clawdy

every week Aunt Claudia traveled to Clayton
first by Hodiamont trolley, then by county bus
and a two mile walk to clean a white woman's house
every week she complained moaning low
like Ma Rainey her daily blues
twice a week she made the fourteen mile trip
passing through the gritty end of the city
to the polished picture window sloping lawns
there to be told she had to wear a head rag
so no loose kinks would fall in the soup
or on the shelf with the good silver
Aunt Claudia kept the work that kept her girls
in Harris Stowe Teachers and more than meaty
gristle on the table come Sundays
sometimes she wondered what might have become
of them if her late husband had conquered
his faint heart   she wondered especially
when she saw a colored man loading a wagon
or on a ladder washing windows
when Big Jim died she resolved her girls
would never do day work   taught them
deportment   taught them to wear clean
underwear in case they fell out in the street
said if your drawers fall down just step
out of them and keep moving like a lady
she might have been thinking about Big Jim
that morning when the Hodiamont trolley rammed
a car some drunk left stuck in the tracks
the trolley had little time to stop and where
she was looking out the window she was looking
at the ceiling at the door at the seat tumbling
and all around yelling and scratching to get out
she lay there breathing the metallic air
trying to see what parts of her worked or not
she claimed that's when she heard Big Jim say:
stay stay   just that morning she'd read
in the Post Dispatch about a woman who
had sued the transit company and they paid
she thought about what that money would buy
how this would be her last day to go to Clayton
stay the voice said *stay* so she ripped off her hat

smudged her face with dirt and pulled
her skirt up just enough to show her clean panties
if someone would bother to look real close

Chitlin' Circuit

Viola played the piano long fingers
skimming keys like sparrows
swarming in the light of dusk

fingers pretty as butterflies and I wondered
how she kept her left hand moving while
her right went off in another direction

my mother said: *making all that racket*
while Viola sang: *I guess I'll have to change
my ways* and threw back her head rocking

until that piano trembled until my mother called me
out of the room: *no piano for you* she said
white folks think that's all we can do

her voice soprano clear and so afraid
of who might hear while Viola
never afraid took her voice

to far away places mostly South
careful back in the day when signs
posted told colored folks where

to go and how long to stay
the family fussed for months wrote letters:
stay here where folks look after you

even after Viola stopped coming home
after she stopped bringing a few
crumpled dollars to fill her mama's kitchen

and stopped telling stories of how
the troupe sped away from some back—
water town in the dead of night to shake

the sheriff's hounds and how once
she thought she saw Son standing
on the last car of the Wabash Limited

letters came for a bit even after she changed
her name *passing* Claudia said and my mother humming
one of the songs she played: *making a whole lotta racket*

Kin Folk

Aunt Maud was so big even Claudia
said she was two axe handles wide

in 1948 she took the train from Texas to visit
reserved the entire row of seats in the colored section

sleeping car porters made way for her in coach
called her Mama Maud as was her due

when she crossed the border into Louisiana
she said she looked back at Texas laughing: *at last I'm free*

she settled all 400 pounds of herself on grandma's horsehair sofa
her seersucker dress spread like a garden of bluebells and peonies

when she handed out pictures of folks back in Texas
everybody talked about who looked like who

how even the ones they couldn't remember
white and colored alike looked like family

they argued whether family mixed Creek Seminole or Chickasaw
and laughed at whites who tried to set themselves apart

you can't spit for hitting one of us Aunt Maud said
Aunt Jennie waved a snapshot of a woman on a porch

so pale she seemed to blend into the clapboards behind her
wanted to know if it was Maud with a tea tray beside her

needs a little toning up to see her Aunt Jennie said
the photo passed from hand to hand in grunted recognition

until Aunt Maud claimed it as the sheriff's mother
blood will tell she said *big boy of hers come huffing*

to get my property like I'm no relation to them—big fool
and all the women started fanning the St. Louis heat

I wouldn't put it past them Aunt Jennie said
Lord a mercy my grandmother mumbled and I

not big enough to stand much taller than Papa's hip
swallowed a giggle each time Aunt Maud said *big*

the talk drifted into how surprised white folks
were to know colored folks could tell

where we came from and who was kin or not
Aunt Maud said she made the sheriff back down

else she'd open all the bedroom windows with a load
of legal papers as to why most folks shared the same

last name and breathed the same foul backwater air
and when my mother nudged me toward her

I watched Aunt Maud's breathing the rising and falling
of beads strung around her neck cradled in the mounds

of her breast like so many stones on a river bank
she opened her arms so I could give her some sugah

I could only see her sitting on that porch swing
made of box springs without the mattress

the sheriff and his dogs yelping to get away
and me lost in a forest soaked in the scent of violets

Immersion

the men are talking quietly
about times so hard getting harder
how even CCC camp didn't ease
the burden of doing twice as much
to get half as far as any white—
the men are talking about olden
days when any black runaway
who sought plantation freedom
followed in darkness the vagrant
stars across the heavens
how different then when death
was sure with whip or gun
fear cleansed by the coolness
of a river or a north wind
deliverance resting on a fuzzy
map half forgotten—
the men who dare are talking
about those men branded
by the system—they talk Jackie
Robinson Paul Robeson and Joe Louis
they talk Jesse Owen
fastest man in the West
they say and pop their suspenders
the men are talking spunk
and guts and who was outsmarted
and who left eating dust—
the men are talking about running
the road legit or not
how under that porter's suit
they are still men answering
to the call of *Boy*—hands washed
clean under sparkling white gloves—
A. Phillip Randolph's men
coming home talking *jack*
about cities they half saw
from a freight or the back
of a dining car between plates
going in and out of galley smoke
changing a bunk or spotting a man
running the tracks—yard dogs
snarling inside his head

the men are putting on their home
suits sitting with ease
their backs against the wall

Uncle Brother

the only boy to survive a string
of girls dying early—a phalanx of doting
sisters who called him Brother
and me—the only grandchild
who survived a generation
of being an only child—the stakes
were high—the only boy who thought
himself the only child flanked by all those sisters
and me the target for his judgments
the girl child my Uncle Phillip named *Joe*
when Uncle Brother didn't have a name
for me at all—I am the one who spied on him
when he brought home a wife from Fort Ord in '44
a woman already a mother who lost all her battles
with Brother's sisters—a woman
without a name I remember—forever known
as *"that woman from California"*
seen not hide nor hair of her since
and Claudia signifying "Brother looked like he didn't
know whether to shit or go blind"
and somewhere in there I became
the patsy for Uncle Brother's stupid
knock-knock jokes—the one who
scrubbed the stairs behind his white
glove inspection—his only real task
to remain the heir apparent
to the family's misfortunes

Top Kick

after thirty years he mustered out of the service—kept his uniform stored in plastic starched clean and ribbons attached—insisted that his civvie shirts should be inspection straight and pant legs parade ready—he talked around his army career never direct but made it clear that when the war in the European Theater moved from west to east he had moved from the motor pool to the front line—there white boys wrote *Kilroy was here* to claim their space and the mess cook stayed pissed off all day—the tanks he serviced were massive hulks that too often made it only a few miles from debarkation before they fell under enemy fire—Patton would have none of that he muttered—he had all the hash marks and stripes to prove his point and even boys in the neighborhood called him *Sarge* out of respect—he knew how to do things right and do them once for effect—shifted into civilian life as if the only thing on his mind was the lawn or the laundry or all the errands to run—that's what he was doing one grey Saturday morning following his wife until he felt thirsty—when she went to the farmer's market he walked into a bar—no joke a colored veteran walked into a bar on the waterfront and asked for a drink—silence until the barkeep said: *we don't serve your kind in here*—he was puzzled at first trying to figure out how to subtract thirty years from this offense—finally he left the bar walked back to his car and returned minutes later—this time he placed his service revolver on the counter and said: *HE needs a drink*—the barkeep flipped a glass quick and filled it brimful with one hand triggering the alarm button under the bar with the other—he stood at attention this man my father—politely thanked the bartender holstered his gun in his belt and downed the shot in one gulp—straightened his tie and readied himself for the cops and his wife

The Thief of Time

on heavy work days Papa wore
his dungarees and cleat boots
traded his Sunday fedora for a watch cap

Mama flat ironed all his shirts
and even polished his lunch bucket
until it was shiny as a new penny

Papa told her to stop but she gave him
the look and kept on going
when Papa was away I'd look

for signs of him—the wood
smell in the chifferobe where
his shaving basin leaked

the ink well in his desk where
he signed papers he said gave us
books and leather shoes

on work days when Papa loaded
the wagons he came home
smelling like sour milk and coal oil

those times he might be gone for days
coming back just before dawn
bringing with him the night chill and fog

Mama was used to his comings
and goings and never told him
some nights she sat up in the window

seat and watched the road below
my mother and her sisters worried
the stories of where Papa might have gone

and when Papa took me to see the Clydesdales
at Anheuser Busch they asked all kinds of questions:
what did you see? who did you see?

what was there beside the horses?
I said the only thing I saw beside the horses
was the feeding wall and water buckets

Papa smiled and hugged me
our secret he winked
one day Papa left and never came back

Aunt Jennie said he took the train west
to see his brother and Aunt Claudia grunted
spread the *Post Dispatch* newspaper

to a story about G-men raiding a brewery
over in Illinois but Mama said
Papa didn't go to Illinois anymore

my mother said: "Something's rotten
in Denmark" and took to her bed
with one of her headaches

I played the Victrola record of Florence Mills
singing: *I'm a little blackbird waiting*
for a bluebird too until the needle broke

when word came Papa died on the train
coming back from California
the women got quiet and folks

from the neighborhood
brought food for the wake
days later two white men

from the brewery showed up
Mama took the pension money
but didn't give them the time of day

Saturday Nights

Papa's girls had all manner of hair
baby fine tendrils that fell tick tack on the floor
ropy coils loosened from rough poufs of hair

by late afternoon the kitchen smelled
of bergamot oil and rosewater steamy
like starch stuck to the flat iron

each argued about who could fix
one another's hair best while the hot comb sizzled
to the click clack beat of curling tongs

Mama said in slavery times every
little girl's hair was cut short to keep folks
from guessing what man had fathered her

like it mattered when the wagon came
to trundle off those sold down the road
their mamas left crying in the dust

they used stingy dabs of Madame CJ Walker's
salve remembering Viola whose baby fine hair
was burnt to the root by backwater beauticians

they spoke of Dora Emma's crinkly hair
a thick braid down her back and stone gray
and Fanny's flapper bangs cut razor straight

they talked queens like Nefertiti and Sheba
they talked fast gals and saints and Broadway Blackbirds
like Ethel or Josephine: *come from St. Louie like us*

when all was said and done they burned the dredges
swept the matted hair into a pie tin leaving
brown marks where the kinky knots had been

so rats wouldn't make a nest of it
so no one could make a nappy wig of it
so no-good folks wouldn't put a spell on them

they cleaned the kitchen with talk of possibilities
of corn rows and spit curls and crimps of hair
bursting out like corks from champagne bottles

A Rightful Place

my mother said when she was young
she'd go to the main library with her sisters
they took three trolleys downtown to the building
with big grey stone lions standing guard

they wore their best Sunday whites
but still the librarians stalked them
through the stacks asking them to repeat
again and again the Dewey Decimal

call numbers for each book they wanted
then pointing to the book and standing
back so the librarian could retrieve it
already they had taken the precaution

of gloves spotless as Sunday dresses
hair ribbons tied in a great bow spread
precise as butterflies leaving the cocoon
and though they spoke in complete sentences

and honored the predicate of subject and verb
careful to never end a sentence in a preposition
they were asked to review their reading habits
before they settled under the low hanging lamps

curious the librarians said that such colored girls
desired to read Shakespeare and chemistry
sorting the books and stopping the longest
on those with the logic of mathematics

the big ones Aunt Fanny requested and
every week the same comment: *this is for boys*
and every week the librarian waited
while Papa's girls readied themselves

for their rightful place among books
until the librarian left them and then
they looked for Dumas and de Maupassant
tales of adventure and romance

that they read sitting straight and proper
the sigh of pages whispering the dance
of geometrical shapes of light through stained glass
like doorways opening for that first kiss

Sunday Best

before Aunt Jennie joined Visitation
Catholic Church I walked Mama

to Lane Tabernacle CME and settled her
in a pew next to Aunt Ethel

the two of them demure in small
pancake hats with fragile veils

among the grand feathered hats of the ladies
who hid a week's worth of bad hair earned

in hot kitchens or sweaty laundries
the ladies of Visitation were all but hidden

in stained glass windows incense and stations
of the cross, their dresses as dull as nun's habits

at Lane Methodist Mama and her sister
sat together their heads tilted toward each other

hats pinned to clouds of kinky white hair
around them ladies in gingham and worn coats

fanned away the heat that had kept them all week
in white kitchens or scrubbing office floors

all week they had been no more than
wallpaper seen and never heard

come Sunday when they sang Amen, feathers
and flowers nodded along with them

when I was older I went with Aunt Jennie
to mass at Visitation, rosary beads matching my dress

on my head a white lace handkerchief pinned
into my curls, my missal white to match

around me ladies of varying hues cradled
their rosaries and echoed a prayer of redemption

come Sunday we were all of the same cloth
women who sought to be what we dreamed

The Weight of Silence

1.

when I was eight the world was neither round
nor flat its borders beginning at Taylor
ended on Ash Hill near the cemetery
where white folks were buried
we lived in the center on Kennerly Avenue
in the last railroad house midblock
on the steepest stretch of the street

at the bottom of the hill the whites only
school stayed safe behind a wrought iron fence
when we went sledding down the hill
I came home with ash gravel
stuck in my knees from falling
Mama would say: *don't disturb the dead*

2.

Mama muttered about the dead the way
my mother muttered about food rationing stamps
both worrying how much the war would take
I eavesdropped from my perch under the table
oak with a support crossbeam where I sat
spying on the women's conversations

in winter the potbellied stove was kept hot
by spring the ashes had been cleared and dumped
in the pit behind the house where they stayed
until the truck from the city picked them up
already it was June and the ashes had cooled
to crystals that crackled when Bumpsy
threw rocks from the garage roof

3.

I was eight that June four years before
Aunt Ethel's son got his degree in dentistry
on account of his bum leg that kept him home
from the war and two years before Uncle Brother
mustered out of the service for unruly behavior

I was eight when Sadie's mama moved in
downstairs with two kids and a piano
a wire thin woman who wore lace collars
her husband she said missing in the Pacific
I waited months to hear her play that piano
something airy leaving the keys tinkling like bells
but always the stairwell was filled with silence

4.

by June Bumpsy and Priscilla (we called her Pussy)
whistled me down the stairs into all day games
of hopscotch and jacks and songs
about smallpox and witches and highwaymen
Sadie was four—thin light skin like her mama
and the boy almost two held tight to her hand
dangled there like a live teddy—we let them play
in the hopscotch chalked permanently on the sidewalk
or with a loose set of jacks lost in the cracks
near the stair well or by the rope tree we climbed
then one day Sadie was gone and her brother
silent scrubbed the chalk in circles

5.

we didn't notice Sadie missing until her mother
screamed like some dog howling on a full moon
neighbor women came to their front doors
then crossed the street to quiet Sadie's mother
already bringing pots of wild greens or beans
still simmering in the juice of ham hocks and onions
cornbread yellow as marigolds on a bright summer day

the women sent us looking but we found nothing
even when Bumpsy ran out of the cemetery
after he heard an owl hooting in daylight
when Papa came home he called the cops
we waited but they didn't come till nightfall
supper for once was quiet that evening

6.

Mama who never talked about the babies she lost
the little ones gone before their first year ended
went searching for a photo of Jessie a middle child
lost in the flu epidemic when she was nearly ten
my Aunt Jessie would forever be a child
staring at the camera—her diploma in one hand

Mama stared at the photo a look my mother held at times
not at but through whatever was right in front of her
while Mama held the photo up to the light
my mother started cleaning the table
though she'd already cleaned twice
Mama, Jessie's dead and gone she said
and I thought I heard Mama say *not gone from me*

7.

I looked at the photo to see some shadow
of my mother in Jessie's face
Jessie standing big eyed in a white blouse
and pleated skirt hanging just so
the bow in her hair spread wide as a halo
her smile as hopeful as the diploma she held
I wanted to know how old she was
I wanted to know if she could
jump rope or play hop scotch
I wanted to know if she ever smiled
then Papa said we had to find little Sadie
Papa said we couldn't wait for peckerwoods
to come looking up in our neighborhood
for a little colored girl lost who knows where

8.

that night I twisted the Green Hornet ring
I bought with cereal box tops   squeezed it
tight to make it glow green in the dark
to bring Sadie back and maybe Jessie too
the next day Bumpsy found little Sadie
curled up in one of the ash pits
like a squirrel sleeping through winter

the cops came once and then the undertaker
the house was filled with folks bringing more
food and hugging Sadie's mother
they held the funeral in the living room
Aunt Jennie did Sadie's hair and Papa
held up her little brother to kiss her goodbye
in her satin bed hair ribbons stiffly in place
sister sleeping he said and Papa nodded *yes*

9.

six months later Papa was dead too
each of his daughters had a different reason
for his death: stabbed one said
shot said another a little hole in his chest
poisoned from the bad food white folks serve
I was told to be quiet: *don't disturb the dead*
Aunt Claudia even said Sadie's mama
had brought the shadow of death
to our house with her fatherless children
the wind hummed in the potbellied stove
the neighbor's dog barked at nothing
all I know is that when I was eight death
came barreling through our neighborhood
and took what I remembered most that year

Rough Trade

my first school year Mildred was paid to walk me twenty blocks to Simmons

Mildred was my play sister until she got interested in boys

she explained where we were and how fast we had to walk to be on time

we walked down Newstead where gypsy cabs and fast gals cruised

union taxis stayed away: *white folks scared of rough trade* my mother said

Mildred's cousin drove a gypsy cab and he was paid to take me home

my mother talked to him for a long time before she decided to trust him

even then Mama wasn't sure: *no telling who's watching that child* she said

Mildred said *look down* when we passed the pool hall and the sanctified church

my eyes watered when their doors were open in the morning to air things out

somebody swept to music pounded on the piano at the sanctified church

that piano set me and Mildred walking faster giggling all the way

even faster when we smelled sour mash odors soaked into the pool hall floor

some days we ran to Taylor Avenue but Anna was upset when I got winded

my mother said she picked Simmons because my cousin Anna taught there

she warned me to call her Miz Davis and not Sweet or Anna like family

Mildred said Simmons was the closest school for colored children

don't matter if Cote Brilliante's down the block all colored children got to walk

as soon as we arrived Anna was there, smiling with both dimples showing

she smelled of talcum powder the scent following her everywhere

I always called her Miz Davis in case some bad girl off Newstead was looking

Immutable Geography

Step on a crack and break your mother's back

in a blighted city, I can not find my past
sidewalks lay in rubble, curbs crumbled
every house I ever lived in torn down
the farmer's market gone, the trolley depot
paved over from Hodiamont tracks to the wharf
whole blocks have turned into war zones
riddled with Berlin blight in the heartland circa 1949
close to the road chain link fences replace
thick privet hedges that once swallowed traffic sounds
Kingshighway no longer holds cars at bay

I can not find my way along unfamiliar roads
gone the drug store where a dentist pulled teeth for free
the last boarded up White Castle a lonely sentinel
lost in the ragged intersection of a food desert
where is the lot my grandmother used to teach me to pick
dandelion greens and mustards chicory and stringy peppers
to add to the pot of 25¢ fatback cooked before my mother
came home from her postwar job at the laundry

what was once a vacant lot or two now knits
even the best blocks of front porch houses
postwar cottages have collapsed upon themselves
tenements shuttered like blind giants
where coltsfoot and chickweed ate brittle grass
that black lawn boys groomed with pinking shears
before the all-white Veiled Prophet Ball began
only the waters of the Wedding of the Rivers
in front of Union Station run at the same sullen rate

I have lost my bearings—search for old man Farrow's
grape arbor where blue black muscadines hung fat
as cherry tomatoes and sweet rocket mixed
with wood sorrel mallow and alfalfa
Farrow's store is gone the barrel of kosher pickles
gone and the wind uninterrupted by the sound
of milk bottles scooped from front stoops
the city has grown raggedy as Lil'Orphan Annie
after Daddy Warbucks left town leaving behind
a river clogged with rich debris unspent
and I have come home furious and wild
faltering along the way

Paint Me Visible

in a family of beautiful intelligent and profoundly
crazy women   one danced in the dark
to soothe her nerves   another wove shawls
from her husband's hair and discarded both
when the work was done   another read palms
tea leaves cards anything that left an imprint
on her inner eye   neighbors said she saw
things nobody else could describe

Lord knows not every family has an oracle or two
women who could hoard love like pirates' treasures
wool gatherers   omen givers   ones who stir
the soup of memory always in their favor   the oldest
daughter the most formidable commanding the others
but you child grew up believing they all held magic
eyes in the back of their heads that told them
what you planned to do before you did it   and you
thinking any one of those women could be your mother
you the child half hidden in the folds of their skirts

Lost Baby Blues

In the family I am neither daughter nor granddaughter
I am what was placed in my mother's arms one night
I call my grandmother: Mama
My family speaks of me in the third person
I am what was placed in my mother's arms one night
Her sisters tell her to take care since I will take care
When she is old but I don't know if she listens
She speaks of me in the third person
Scolds me by my full name
Even when she knows I am not listening
I call my grandmother: Mama
Even though she tells me she is not my mother
Every day my mother scolds me
Calls me out of my name so I'll listen
Her sisters tell her I will take care of her later
My mother is not listening
She is scolding me for every breath I take
I was put in her arms during twilight sleep
She boasts: I didn't feel a thing
I am the thing she did not feel
She tells me I should feel grateful
I am grateful she has only one brother
His arms grow tired when he hits me
All these girls and one boy: grandma complains
My mother's complaints are louder
I am not her daughter not granddaughter
I am only what was placed in her arms one night

What the Body Remembers

a fost ō dotā (there was a time)

shoes my first conscious thought my second birthday present

baby white lace ups so white they swallow light

Aunt Ethel's building ringed by metal catwalks

Mama sitting on the sofa with her sister Aunt Ethel

my mother sitting in a chair next to me

my mother tugging at my clothes so I'll look nice

Aunt Ethel a darker version of Mama hiding behind her glasses

tea and cookies served in the living room

cookies and milk for me until full I squirm in the chair

my mother brushing cookie crumbs off my dress

my mother pushing me out the door onto the gangway

I watch light fall through the metal grating

I watch doors open and close on floors above and below

I try listening to the women talk to Aunt Ethel

my mother shoves me away from the door I jump up jump up

to show I am unhappy the sound of my shoes grates against the gangway

I jump again and sound travels from the grating to the garden

I give one more kick and my mother comes to the door

Aunt Ethel and Mama right behind her as she screams

the black streak of metal across the white leather from toe to heel

the sound of the gangway still ringing in my ears

Home Remedies for Children

> coal oil dribbled over
> a lump of sugar cures anything . . .
>
> —*The Book of Home Remedies*

by all accounts I was nearly four
before I realized someone was missing
that no account, Claudia would say
she looks just like that man, Jennie would say
my mother nursing another headache I caused
and Mama hustling me out of the room

I asked Papa who said, *never you mind*
as if that could keep me from listening at key holes
or close my ears when I hid under the table
never you mind was the only way I would mind
my questions of *where is he* never ceasing

that man never did a thing for you, my mother said
yet they all admitted I had his long legs
and big eyed smile that meant I was thinking
something naughty to plague them even as
I was leaving the room leaving as he did

if Papa's not my daddy where is my daddy, I asked
gone, my mother said *he'll be back*, Mama said
no account, Claudia said and Jennie helped sort
the gifts that arrived in the mail addressed to me
regular as clockwork for birthdays and Easter
the savings bonds my mother kept for when we
would need them except we did not mean me

I have to admit through it all I was spoiled
as if I was a wanted child my battles generational
no sibling rivalry at all no squabbles about who
would set the table or mop before Uncle Brother came
tripping up the steps   no one but me to do chores
not with me being the only one there
the shadow of my birth father stuck in the doorway

Precocious

my mother is angry with me
I am barely four just young enough
to get on the bus for free
but my mother is angry with me
when I read aloud the bright
placards curved high
above the bus windows
I read aloud the placards
asking us to buy nothing
that is free and my mother
grows angry as I read
everything I can barely see
I want to tell her letters
go all mushy melting together
before my very eyes
but my mother is angry
when the bus driver tells her
she must pay for me since
children who are truly young
can not read the ads they see
my mother yanks my collar
tells me *sit be still*
you'll ruin your eyes
reading everything you see
she threatens to put me
in school a year before
I'm ready and I smile
my mother frowns and asks
what will become of me
if I insist on reading
every little thing I see

The Answers to Why

because her daughter, Claudia, had babies while Mama
was still having babies   family lines blurred

mothers and daughters waltzing just out of reach

because her daughter, Jennie, turned Catholic
Mama took me to Lane Methodist each Sunday

because a photographer penciled an outline
around Mama's cottony hair Jennie studied

tinctures and rouges any one-eyed camera could find

because she could not read Mama memorized
all the songs in the hymn book

the communion wine tasted like grape juice

because Mama fed me from a bowl that read: *find the bottom*
I ate my vegetables sipped pot liquor while she sang old time songs

spoon to mouth: *Ol'Dan Tucker too late to git his supper*

because Mama's fingers grew thick in winter
I learned to braid her hair

because Mama got too old to do *fine work* as she called it
I became her eyes to thread needles and pick loose hems

I made sure the white butcher didn't put his thumb on the scale

because my mother, Ruth, worked at Fort Leonard Wood
Mama taught me how to cook

what's a Leonardwood? I asked

because my mother opened mornings like a can of beans
fussing and cussing and quoting Shakespeare

between dammit-I'll-bite-you and scrambled eggs

because Mama said my mother was moody and needed help
I watched my mother paint fake stocking seams down her legs

shapely as Betty Grable   high heels clicking on the linoleum
heading to the door   factory head scarf tied neat as a Sunday hat

because we had afternoons alone Mama taught me
how to knead bread dough the proper way—knuckles down

because Mama singed her eyebrows when the pilot light
went out Papa bought a brand new stove

I missed the old stove and its stand-up oven

because Papa said none of his girls would do day help
I read the papers and dialed the telephone for Mama

because Papa died on the train coming home from California
Mama sat by the window all day and wouldn't talk

because Claudia had become a widow before Papa died
my mother and her sisters fought to get Mama's attention

because Mama said the four poster was too big
after Papa died I slept with her

in the same bed she'd birthed babies who lived
and those who didn't

I counted angels carved in the chifferobe door

because a spider bit me the first night I slept
in the four poster Mama propped me on pillows

so I wouldn't roll onto the blister on my back

because Mama covered the bite in goose grease
there was no trace of the spider come morning

because the chifferobe held Papa's shaving basin
and shoes I spent hours inspecting the little shelves

because Mama put plugs in the locks of Papa's
roll top desk and chifferobe I always had a way out

because Mama said there were two places
she wouldn't want to be: hell and west Texas

we lived in that railroad house on Kennerly for years

because Mama didn't trust white people after the Klan
shot the mules dead in front of the old family house

because after they moved to Missouri Mama said she saw
ghosts walking the long hallway that banked the house

because she said it so much I thought I saw them too
and my mother said *don't talk about the old ways Mama*

because my mother worked long days I learned Mama's stories

because Mama lived in the past when Papa was alive
and lived every day when he wasn't she couldn't stop

because my mother caught Mama telling me stories
of the time before Lincoln freed us my mother argued

but Mama said she had to tell me what was just because

The Legacy

> Behind every man now alive stand 30 ghosts, for that is the ratio by which the dead outnumber the living
>
> —*2001: A Space Odyssey*

my mother and I walk between rows of clothes she stored in the basement
my inheritance collected from her siblings who died at least a decade ago

each garment she says still worth years of wear as she mentally measures
my height and weight for suits double-breasted and dresses saved for Sunday

wire hangers click against the metal rods as we move from one garment rack
to the next checking the tales she conjures of who wore what and when

her test for me come home again from *God knows where* she says
as if she marvels I've come home at all and can remember anything

the basement smells of must and mold the air turned thick and gray
our footsteps on the concrete floor become a muffled sigh against

good clothes saved for special occasions—prêt-a-porter for any passerby
the rustle of garments on each rack now gathers the dust of neglect

remember this? my mother asks pulling out a yellow dress
I want to tell her I remember even when I don't

I want to say that was the dress Aunt Jennie wore when she taught
me how to set a dining table like *Good Housekeeping* magazine

I want to say that was the dress Aunt Claudia wore in a photo
of her sitting next to Aunt Ethel who was brown as Papa's whiskey

instead I blurt out *you cursed yellow when I was twelve*
remembering how the curse so strong I still bristle at the thought

my mother doesn't mention how I defiant climbed a fence and tore
the brand new dress regardless of the cost of it the color or the fit

she dips into her bag of quotes and whips me with a Shakespeare
barb: *through tattered clothes great vices do appear* and I

become once again the child with no defense my face poker straight
as she sorts what we might stomach from what leaves a bitter taste

Learning to Love Bessie Smith

took years by all accounts cause
who could love a whiskey voice
lamenting some no-good man
and Aunt Claudia hissing *yes*
like an untethered balloon
when Sweet her daughter said *plenty do*
and my mother wouldn't even entertain
the possibility given
how she had no call to trust
any man aiming to separate her
from the family
and I just flat out couldn't understand
what all that weeping was about
while I tried sneaking
a taste of cherry spiked drink
tried listening as Aunt Jennie said
baby, men come on like busses
another stop along by and by
Jennie a little tipsy
filling everybody's cup
until the punch bowl emptied
and my mother eating all the fruit
because she didn't drink when
for a time she was single again
waiting by the side of the road

My Mother's Baby Toe

Her foot bore the mark of her brother's mischief
baby toe crooked like the head of a cane
some inches apart from the rest of the foot.
Until the toe settled into its awkward shape
she learned to walk despite the pain
never told anyone how deliberate her brother
had been at twisting until he heard it crack.
And even then Uncle Brother could do no wrong
he the last child the only boy in that chorus
of girls and she the one right before him—
the youngest of Papa's daughters and darkest
among her sisters all fair with a kiss of brown.
Brother aquiline and fair as well
the baby to boot who answered to none.
What to say when all the older sisters
adored him and to say adored was not enough
say cooed and cuddled praised his every move
my mother's toe her secret reliquary.

Did You Ever Have the Feeling

> You knew it was right, wasn't wrong.
> Still you knew you wouldn't be very long
>
> —*Jimmy Durante*

my mother said when I was born
Mama told Uncle Brother his sister
had given birth to a baby girl
Uncle Brother asked if he could
have another helping of chicken
that's how it was between us
he the prince and me the mouse
in the corner squeak squeaking
with my crayons and books

        Mopping the entry hall stairs my worst chore ever
        Rag mop & bucket soap & wood tip it & I'm done for

some said Brother's nose was his best feature
that is to say his nose was his biggest feature
the same shaped nose his sisters had
seemed odd on him below his wolf beige eyes
Romanesque if you looked at the history
books in the downtown library and believe me
I looked and looked but even with dirty
glasses could not imagine Uncle Brother
reining in a chariot   neighbor women
argued that he looked like the Indian
head embossed on the nickel
more like Jimmy Durante I thought

        He followed me with white gloves & the geometry
        Of stairs: begin again mop to wood risers to step

folks said Uncle Brother had a handsome face
and though they may have thought it
none ever said he was a handsome man
cause who would think that skinny boy
with a riot of sisters was a man anyway
when he couldn't even keep up with work
in the WPA and that was all designed
by the gov'ment for poor folk like us
Brother's allergic to trees, my mother said

The third time something told me I had to go
At the same time I knew that I had better stay

for years Uncle Brother seemed always to be
leaving or just returning wearing out his welcome
where he was too smart to do day labor
and too stubborn to obey orders
even the talent agents in L.A. said he could be
a stand-in for George Raft in the right light
the story goes that he opted out for a stalk of bananas
eating his way one bunch at a time in one day
until he was discharged for disorderly behavior
Brother always had a delicate stomach my mother said

Start to go again & change your mind again
Do, re, mi, fa, so . . . let it go

the last time I saw Uncle Brother I was fifteen
and he was standing at the top of the stairs
checking my work with those damn white gloves
that told him three tries and the job still undone
I cursed him because my mother loved him
more than me and when he slapped me
I slapped him back with the rag mop
a satisfying *splat* that left him dripping
dirty water down his starched shirt
get your skinny butt back here he yelled
as I slammed the door: *Go or stay, stay or go:*
not the exit I'd always planned when
in my teenage dreams I stood by the door
Papa's fedora cocked to one side as I waved
ha-cha-cha straight up Durante style

Chevalier

my mother said the first time Uncle Phillip
saw me he called me *Joe* and the name stuck
when he stroked my cheek I reached up
grabbed his little finger hung on
for dear life he said *Hey Joe*
and I smiled *Indigestion* my mother said

his greeting made me feel grown up
even when I was five and after the war years later
he took the job he said Uncle Sam had trained
him for during his four years in Quartermaster
even when Aunt Jennie protested
that no husband of hers should pick up
other people's trash he became the best
never missing a day of work

everyone knew Uncle Phillip had both a steady
job and another family on the other side
of town though Jennie never spoke of either
and Phillip kept his balance easy between
them the same as when he rode harness
on the truck by luck I saw him once out near
Fairground Park and he waved *Hey Joe*

I answered *Hey Uncle Phillip* as he hung
on the running board like a rodeo cowboy
Uncle Phillip the purveyor of cool always dapper
good hair slicked back—tie tack a blazing diamond
spent hours shaping his mustache like Cab Calloway
some Saturdays he'd put on a nickel thick 78rpm
and turn up the volume on the Motorola
when he beckoned me I was beside him
before he could finish saying *Com'on Joe*

once Aunt Jennie tap danced on the hood
of his shiny new coupe raging against the sight
of him riding down Delmar with some other woman
so mad even the white wall tires trembled
Uncle Phillip stood in the doorway watching
laid back as if he were waiting for the mailman
when I squeezed in beside him he winked
his laughter singing to the sun

Aces and Eights

when my father was home on leave
two sounds filled the house:
the slap of cards in one long game
of solitaire and the splash of whiskey
in his ever present glass
cards shuffled in and out like acrobats
and he warned when he caught me
practicing: *play by yourself*
and have a fool for a partner

the year that all the white people ran away
and abandoned Cote Brilliante Elementary
to the neighborhood colored kids
my father came home on a 26 day furlough
he asked me what I liked for lunch
I said bologna sandwich and green peas in milk
for 26 days I had bologna cross hatched
and fried with a side bowl of green peas
the butter still melting the way it looked
on the Del-Monte can in the kitchen
and Mama watching, shaking her head

I learned to count cards by the fourth grade
learned the riffle of a good shuffle
over hand or slide thumbs always inward
seven times seven he instructed
we started with simple games
hearts and black jacks
graduated to poker clean and neat
I the terrible loser mostly weeping

when he swept the miserable pennies
into his palm like marbles and
my week's allowance in his pocket
I had no choice but a quick loan
from my mother's purse
a little not to be missed I thought
but my mother caught me anyway
and daddy made me recite a story
for every card in the deck

I learned to read his drinking moods
blues in the morning gospels in the afternoon
when Nellie Lutcher's *"real gone guy..."*
slid into Mahalia's *"Take my hand, precious Lord..."*
and the gospel spirit commenced to grab him
I quick took charge of the liquid spirits
dealing a new spread of cards
before his despair caught my mother
in the crossfire between blues and retribution

my second year in high school I succumbed
to Famous Artists Draw Me ads on match covers
with my father the easy target for paying the bill
I made my move between random
shuffles and his next shot glass of Kentucky
he said my drawing got the eyes all wrong
but bet me double or nothing
I wouldn't last six months
then poured a thimble of bourbon
an ocean of amber it seemed

he handed me a chili pepper
first take a bite of this, he said
I went all bug-eyed and lurched
across the table making sounds
in some language I had yet to hear
my father raised his glass
Baby, you just understood relativity
but my body was in full rebellion
and nothing much made sense

the next year my father was transferred
again and said this time he received
travel allotments for my mother and me
to live on base instead of some dingy
one-horse town where army folks were trash
we were going to Wyoming he said
and broke a new deck of cards
I thought of Papa and Jackson
the Badlands and red sunsets
my life that would change forever
if the cards were right
and my father stayed sober long enough

Defining Life

we have come to take care of Jennie
three cousins come to tend our auntie
we need her alive since our own mothers
seem unable to bend our disobedient bodies
we have come to a house that reeks
of life barely pushing against death
Jennie hanging between the two
yellowed by jaundice and worn out
we have come two cousins and me
thirteen to fifteen straining at the bit
thinking life is what we count on
groping for words to say so
each morning when we awake
not where we want to be
but now for once agree that here
is where we are supposed to be
two days Jennie has hovered in the soup
of medicine brought home from hospital
to die they said to die
we tend Aunt Jennie our elder
our toughest teacher she the barren
sister of Mama's many children
we sob and weep and wring our hands
walk to the door and back again
what can we do we who know
no more of life than any magazine
then we see her eyelids flutter
a voice so weak surely not hers
a hoarse crackle that fills the air
I'm not dead yet
and we stumble over our own
feet ready to do her bidding
adding to our vocabulary
the word: remission

Lessons in Deportment

1.

for over a year I lived at Aunt Jennie's
with my cousins, the two Jeans

all of us having run away from our mothers
to the safety of Jennie's Victorian style house

and in my case safe from Uncle Brother too
one-two-three we arrived motherless homeless

here comes another one just like the other one
and Aunt Claudia saying all us girls being there

could only mean Jennie was running a house
like Aunt Dora Emma had that time back

during Prohibition *split tails come in here
looking like first one thing then another*

Aunt Jennie was having none of it
called Claudia a box-ankle heifer

and dared her to repeat what she had said
Claudia didn't come to sit a spell for weeks

2.

Jennie, the aunt with no children, took us
girls ripening into our teens come calling
between pee pants and first periods

house rules Jennie said *no sass no lip*
and none of us allowed to treat her
like she was our mother and our *yes ma'am*

sounding too weak and practiced
Jennie staring dead at us for the longest time
before she said we were too dumb to see the difference

between a salad fork and a nose pick
so every night one of us would set the table
with more silverware than we'd ever use

begin with the one nearest the plate
she told us and moved us from chowing
down hobo style to sitting for our supper

we cleaned up nice by Saturday
left the kitchen neat and tidy
heading for the Y to belly rub at the sock hop

3.

the Jeans and I hated doing laundry
so we hid dirty clothes all over the house

under cushions in closets under the beds

one morning we woke up to Jennie raging:
pulling down curtains, tearing off bed sheets
throwing towels and anything washable

in a pile that she pointed to yelling:
you will not leave this house until
everything is clean as Sunday, hear me?

this time we said *yes ma'am*
with bowed heads and a silent prayer
that she'd found all the clothes

all the time wondering how a woman
of so much heft could move so fast

4.

she lined us up in the basement
    like army recruits—me the oldest

at the head of the line followed
    by the two Jeans: one-two-three

wash-rinse-press! she ordered
    we looked at the Maytag wringer

the scrub board and steam press
    we looked at the basement walls

blistered with sweat and the morning
    sun not yet clearing the top

of the oak tree in the back yard
    how could we make it to noon?

to this day I don't even throw clothes
    away without cleaning them first

5.

one afternoon Aunt Jennie found me
reading a Prince Valiant comic book

she snatched it from me before
I could convince her it was history

knights of the Round Table and all that
go in there and read Papa's books

she said and pushed me
toward the leather bound volumes

ready for the taking
and so many words to capture

the two Jeans peering
between the crack of the sliding door

snickered about homework
avoided by all but the spineless

keep rolling your eyes Jennie said dismissing
those who didn't apply themselves to study

6.

a year earlier when my mother moved
into a new house with Uncle Brother
taking everything Mama had owned with Papa
Aunt Jennie pried Papa's books away from Claudia
got it hand over fist she grinned

I remembered the shiny leather books
in the room with the horsehair sofa
where I could look but never touch
and the tapestry on the wall above
of some place far far away

after Papa died I'd go into that room
lie down on the floor and dream of
myself on the desert of the tapestry

I imagined its secrets were hidden
in those books and read ravenously

one day Jennie suggested that I should
think about college maybe Xavier
where she had attended fitting in
with light skin girls

the sliver of light between the sliding
doors blinked for a moment

not me I thought and held up my hand
two shades darker than hers
two shades darker than a paper bag
child there are other schools she said

I imagined that stretch of desert
on the tapestry and crossed my fingers

7.

baby life is hard Jennie said *you've got to make*
yourself presentable   I was sitting on her bed
watching her dress for work   a new job

where she said she had to look healthy
if she wanted to keep from getting fired
in case her sickness returned

we didn't know then she'd last another 50 years
she pointed to her stockings
I lifted the flimsy things while she struggled

with the last few inches of a Playtex girdle
encasing her like a sausage
the closest I came to my mother's underwear

was staring at the pink rubber douche bag
hanging limp on the bathroom door
I was 90 pounds fully clothed and soaking wet

but Claudia wanted me to wear a girdle
I saw where the latex pinched Jennie's flesh
as she snapped her stockings in place

done and done she said and turned around
her pleated skirt brushing against
her calves and crackling with static

8.

Aunt Jennie was a clothes horse from head to toe
the sad little clothes I cut for paper dolls

when I was in grammar school gathered dust
in a shoe box at my mother's house

at Jennie's I had the real thing
and the best model to show off

satins and velvets and real suede shoes
with slanted heels sometimes worn

for no occasion at all except
she liked the feel of them that day

once we had a family barbeque
in the back yard   two pits Uncle Philip

and my father manned like admirals in the thick of it
Jennie wore a satin pants suit *like Joan Crawford*

rushing from smoke that blew her way
I had helped her dress that morning

watched her wrap her hair in a wire rat
neat as pie crust at the nape of her neck

the day before she had lost her job
politics she told me and gave me

the glad eye then danced with Uncle Philip
as if she had all the riches in the world

The Spinisters

when Anna Mae fell in love working
in the munitions factory Claudia
snatched her eldest daughter home
determined as she was for Anna
not to fall prey to men with silk suits
and suede tongues the men who called
her Sweet instead of Anna

and Claudia who had never been a girl
who had gone from child to mother
tending all the children her mother birthed
sent Anna to Harris-Stowe Teachers
where she could *make something of herself*
where she learned to lead classrooms
of children so like the one she had lost

Claudia's youngest daughter Modestine
wanted to be another Rosie the Riveter
during the war but after her sister's escapade
she settled for learning the speed
of typewriters sitting upright and straight
according to books on etiquette for girls
she counted on listening to juke boxes
instead of counting words per minute

Modestine not so modest became Tina
and counted on a diamond ring
flirting with a young boy from Texas
his skin almost the color
of his wing tip brogans and Tina
almost got that ring before Claudia
sent both ring and bearer packing

both of Claudia's sons married beautiful women
she hated their wives for their sweet dispositions
her daughters became women living
with lost dreams growing plump
as chocolates in a See's candy box
growing stale locked in the house
wearing bright red lipstick
matching house coats and minks
and their mother reminding them
they didn't need a man for this

Breaking Wild Horses

for Anna and Modestine

Claudia's youngest daughter
read romance novels constantly
she said in one of her stories
when romance walked in
there were too many fatal secrets
hiding in sheltered places
the heroine tried roping them in
corralling their savage cries
for attention—nothing seemed
to hold them at bay especially
as night broke the skyline
and her guard was down

no one would tell her these stories
had become her-story the history
of fences rattling with weakness
the whinny and stomping
of half remembered injuries
and families scabbed over.
she fussed with the images
trying to tidy them into civil
obedience—read how others
had calmed their unruliness
with whispers that could not be heard
as they nuzzled soft places
left trails of rancid breath
flicked debris into the room (onto the table)

too late she saw romance move on
she sipped small glasses of wine
to ease the ache each story cost
and when she retold the tale
she was at the center when
the old nags came closer to the house
chewed on the lace curtains.
she couldn't just put them down
not after they had been around
so long and carried so much baggage.

so she groomed them boasted about their origins
how difficult it had been to finally
keep them away from her comings
and goings—herded them into a far field
where their passing might go unnoticed

The Fire Inside

the men sit in lawn chairs under the elm tree
the surprise is how many of their photos appear
in a world you thought held only women
where were they when your grandmother
lamented the host of girls she birthed moaning
the stork brought me only one boy child

the men sit in the shadows of the tree
you are told to let them be with their talk
your world populated by women quick
to remind you of your birth father's absence
while page after page of faces recall
a family of men rusted from hard work

men turning into boys dressed
for the camera's occasion
natty suits pressed pin neat
you catalog by the shape of the nose
long and regal for your grandfather
or the slant of eye from great grandmother

no clues from skin color in varying hues
from porcelain to pitch uncles and cousins
seeming to strut while holding still
Son in half shadows his eyes like glittering knives
and Warren a sweet brown version of Widmark
or some Oscar Micheaux film character

those in uniform remind the younger ones
how colored troops were the first
to liberate Dachau and how Patton trusted
his precious tanks to their care
men posed like gangsters or hipsters
leaving behind the ache of racism and riots

for this moment before the camera
their forever buttoned up in a clean shirt
colored only signs smudged in the lens
men folk who earned their place
frozen in time as if with the next breath
they will reveal everything under that mask

Missouri Blues

when Aunt Claudia's oldest joined the police force
the family swayed between pride and fear knowing
they'd already lived through a war where men died

in uniform colored or not and came back home where
colored died in uniform war or not and Aunt Claudia
said if her son was good enough for Uncle Sam

he damn sure was good enough for St. Louis
true James was the only colored they knew to rise so far
so the women figured how fast he could fall

that first year James couldn't find a decent partner
to save his soul as one after another failed him
made him climb fences when the road was clear

chase a cat up a tree to see how high he'd crawl
took bets against his failures always odds against him
my mother asked Claudia if she should dare speak

to James when he was on patrol worried he'd become
like the white ones who entered without invitation
searching every nook and cranny for something

wrong when everything in the house was right
then came the attack at Fairground Park where white boys
beat up colored boys for swimming in the same water

and every precinct in the city on alert white or not
Aunt Claudia out in the hall crying and cussing
walking between the front door and back porch

and Aunt Jennie turning up the radio loud
and everybody knowing that calling it an incident
was a way of saying white folks started the fight

until like turning off a faucet all the women said Claudia
had better fix her face right so James could do his job
colored gone so far but never as far as we wanted to go

Aunt Claudia drew herself up like puffer pigeon
taking a deep breath in the thin air and everybody sat down
waiting for James to come home to family acting like usual

Throwing Stones at the All White Pool

after Gwendolyn Brooks

the first plopped mid-pool
leaving an oh-so shallow cavern
niga niga niga sucking in all
the hooting hollering spit of words
the next volley closer to shore
rippled in eddies of false kindness
lacy little bubbles popping
in warm summer air like flower buds
after that they all joined in willy-nilly
they all silly smiled made fart sounds
with their arm pits as we eased toes in
refused to show hurt that never goes away
we were afraid we were afraid
we'd gone too far to turn back
we owned the pain   broke the barricades
owned up to our small failures
eight year old bodies prickled with icy shocks

Fade to Black

in the Antioch Theater we feasted on films
made by colored folks like Oscar Micheaux
those Saturdays back then when we were Colored
before we were Black and all films were black and white
after Hopalong Cassidy rode into white westerns
we watched Ralph Cooper or Mantan Moreland
break up shady deals in Harlem guns blasting
tables turned against white folks robbed
of their power on the silver screen
at those matinees we cheered always the underdog
even Boston Blackie who was black in name only

between Movietone News and cartoons
we laughed stomped and celebrated in the dark
this was like recess without teachers to boss us

one Saturday I stayed too long at the party
and by nightfall my mother sent my cousins
James and Warren to fetch me—the two entering
like side kicks in one of Micheaux's films
Bumpsy hooted louder than the others
when my name appeared on a slip of paper
inserted between the projector and lens
James in police uniform found me in the beam
of his flashlight and Warren scouting the other aisle

left me no escape but to follow the sheriff out
to the dusky evening where my mother waited
while Micheaux's detectives ran toward the light

Double Dutch

for Valerie

we jumped till dusk
legs and arms glistening
from the vaseline coating
our mothers had faithfully
applied to ward off scrapes
from missteps and fumbled
ropes never dependable::

once upon a time the goose drank the wine

we jumped sally-go-round
and hotpeppers hotpeppers
while boys in highwater pants
cheered us on and the light
shifted as if the Mississippi
wanted to suck in all the sun::

in those days before the days
we joined the band called
raging hormones we jumped
while porch ladies squinted
to measure how high
our skirt tails floated
in the fading light::

the monkey played the fiddle on the street car line

we jumped for the pure
joy of jumping—the best of us
all loosey-goosey between
the whisk of ropes that raised welts::
get back snap snap snap
we did riffs on Mary Mack
and one potato two or no will to stop
jumping until the sting
of burning muscles pulled us down::

the street car broke the monkey got choked

we gauged the space
between the salvo of ropes
crisscrossing above
our heads below our feet
before we danced in
or sashayed out highstepping
our way past danger::

had we but known we could
have woven tales
in the space of ropes
doubled overhand and under
slapslapslapping the ground
as we lost count of insults
and slights and who
black or white was on first::

and all went to heaven but the sanctified folk

in those days we jumped
before we knew what ground
swells waited to suck us in
the litmus test of race and class
and what ropes were no doubt
left waiting to trip us::
we jumped toward the sky
before the night swallowed light
and where else did we have
to go but up

Tongue Tied

they were always talking
the women in my family
                their tongues the most brutal
                muscle in the body taking all
      available space
      all talking
      all at once
confabulating my father said

one day I asked my mother when did she get to be older than my father?
very calmly she answered: a couple of years ago

the most powerful muscle
                in the body
                lies the tongue
      always seeking
      another
fault line to sink
            its teeth into

Uncle Roman's daughter now a mother herself got younger each year
my mother who would hide her own age for nearly a hundred years asked:
how can you be younger than your daughter?
that's her problem my aunt replied

they talked the women
held vigils and rites of passage
                old stories that cut
                to the quick
                a slip of the tongue

Uncle Brother's second wife had a bump on the end of her tongue
a fleshy pearl that appeared and disappeared as she spoke
proving the women said that she was a great liar

they dueled with words

Claudia's cussing could sink a naval fleet
these women holding truth
                    at arm's length
                    trust at bay
          pull a tooth
          and the tongue
aches to fill the space
                    harry-assing my father said

one of the Jean's disappeared for more than a year
when she returned Aunt Jennie forced her to call her mother
who answered: the voice sounds familiar but I just can't place you

best you hold your tongue
around these women
          the tricks they've learned
          to say nothing while talking
                    were taught in the best
                    houses where all surfaces
                    reflected
          every image
          except theirs

after four children bang-bang-bang my Aunt Claudia
gave her last child the middle name *Hope*
to swear she said for hope-no-more children

                                        they spoke the woman
                    of how the thrush of bigotry
                    coats the tongue of how
the tongue curls around
half swallowed words
                    nice nasty verbs
                    that keep the body moving

when I asked a simple question my mother had a grandiose answer: can I go out?
out out brief candle life is but a walking shadow
yes or no would have served me better

the tongue searches

every pocket and crevice
           where sweetness
           can hide
      love melts
      under the tongue
and when the tongue says
love   power grows

whenever I entered a room the women stopped talking family
child, bite your tongue

Twilight Sleep

> The bearing of a child was henceforth to be merely a time of twilight and of sleep.
>
> —*Twilight Sleep: The Dämmerschlaf of the Germans*

that last July before she died
my mother visited every morning
in the twilight of dawn—
she came quietly into my room
arriving in wingless flight
to light upon my bed—I felt her weight
in my half sleep stage and like her
giving birth to me, no other sensation—
a small indentation where she perched
and spoke as if in mid-conversation
her voice spidery as the penmanship
she'd learned as a young girl
the flourishes and serifs of a fountain pen
from a time past when looped cursives
adorned great documents—my mother
spoke in cursives quoting Shakespeare
for any question I'd ask from age three—
that July she sat on my bed
and whispered as if by memory
her lament soft as a lullaby—
I heard only the tone of words
punctuated by my name and
the whisper of her weight
as she turned to leave
the space closing behind her—
I thought she said: I have to go
and strained to hear the lock
catch at the front door
as I awoke alone to silence

The Mistress of Secrets

after Erica Jong

you remember waves rocked the boat
you oared—*MOTHER* stenciled on its side

she was the graffiti artist tagging negatives
in large letters for all the world to see

while you trawled for her attention in a spell
of bad weather some distance from home—

       consider how she filled any room
       with the dead weight of her sadness

       and to think you once adopted her
       demons as your own while you rowed

       so fast you never noticed you'd entered
       dangerous waters—a life unfit

for anything but bad luck—years
later when you called she answered

the phone as if she barely had been
interrupted on some errant party line

you never understood this disconnect
and wanted to tell her how difficult

       the years had been with nothing
       but a trace of her and how like tissue

       paper dress patterns you never got the seams
       right and now want to travel backwards

dodging rogue waves steering as always
toward what passes for love

countless nights you lay awake waiting
for the other shoe to drop some accusation

her sighs picked up the eddies of the Mississippi
turned them cobalt blue slinging mud in all directions

echoing from the next room, next house, next town
the boat tipping dangerously close to water

as if dancing to some pisces keen at eventide
the drift pulling us mother to daughter on this ride

listen she says *listen* then tells you only
what she wants you to know, changing

her age, her weight, what she saw and when
she now tells you the latest storm broke the fence

and how insurance would only cover half
of the tree, the bottom splintered by wind

listen she says but you hear only the gasp
of the last wave out carrying all she left unsaid

The Prodigal Daughter

this is for the blue haired colored ladies who praised
memorization and good posture at all costs

this is for my mother who wrote warnings in Shakespearean
couplets across the mirrors reflecting our image

who every winter saved money to send the blonde
baby dolls her sisters gave me to the doll hospital

so they'd come home brown as toast like me

this is for Warren smart in his uniform fresh from battle in forty-six
who let me tell the high school crowd he was my boyfriend

and this is for his mother Claudia who taught discipline

to her daughters by depriving them of all pleasures—who sold
everything in her mama's house to the junk man for $300

this is for the blues Viola sang her voice salty with urgency
who disappeared into whiteness leaving dancing shoes bunions and all

this is for my grandfather who showed me the Anheuser's
Clydesdales when I was six and he kept the stables clean

this is for my grandmother's chewy dumplings floating
in a fragrant stew of peaches and spice—her stove

with the stand up oven its emblem of a chicken hatching

this is for Mildred who walked me a mile to school while
the one at the end of our block stayed closed to blacks

this is for Jennie's family barbeques—Uncle Phillip lifting
slabs of ribs with the same precision he used to maneuver

city dump trucks—that day we ate *high on the hog*

this is for my mother's spaghetti strap high heels and shorts
her dark brown legs that went on forever—both of which

I inherited—my mother who kept me in fighting
shape for the strange world I would encounter

Lividity

after more than seventy years of marriage
the old wounds never healed

layers of scab scraped
by the next discontent

a casual blow that left
an open sore neglects metastasized

the lesion visible from a distance
that even he now blind could see

the elm tree leaned closer
sap bled into crusty bark

limbs complained to windows
barred against the shade

the sun a mere flash of red
sinking into the evening's impending dark

and she who could not hear knew
when the light would disappear

Did I Know You Back Then?

when I came home wearing a gélè my mother
looked at me as if I were a stranger
my father said *black is beautiful*
my mother insisted I remove the gélè
so she could see all that so-called beauty
and my hair released from the wrap
bounded out in the glossy kinks of an afro

when I came home sporting a brand new
passport and a fellowship to foreign places
my mother's unfolded her litany of warnings
and Jennie gave me her standard caution
best learn to pee in a coca cola bottle
she said remembering the jim crow limits
of traveling across these united states

when I came home with a new husband
not from any branch of our extended relations
my mother's first question as he took
off his coat: *how's your finances?*
my hazel eyed Irishman grinned from ear to ear
and sat down beside my father
to talk military politics and jim beam

when I came home with a PhD
and yet another divorce still fresh my mother
said *they'll find you dead some place*
nobody has ever been while she plucked
imaginary lint from my clothes and hair
the wall behind her chair dedicated to me
adorned with photos drawings awards

when I came home to accept an honor
from a local poetry group my mother
complained that there was no one
in the hotel to look after me   and those
who recognized her as my mother
said she sat in the back row grumbling
about missing dinner as I read each poem

when I came home on a stop over
along a transoceanic route my mother
cooked a box lunch of chicken feet
and rice old style with the toes sticking
up like baby fingers escaping the mire
something for the plane she said
like your granma used to make
pressing the foil wrapped dish in my hand
as if it were the final link to family

each time I came home not enough
or too often too long and might as well not
each time at the arrival gate she tweaked
loose strands of hair   loose threads
all of me out of whack and out of place
the barriers of what kept us at odds
each from the other in the web of our invention
and always I left taking a little of her with me

The Third Stage

when my mother retired as head cashier
at the post exchange she walked
along I-170 to the nearest
mall to buy the week's groceries
suburbs sprawled across the thoroughfare
in all directions with no foot traffic
my mother so pleased to be free
of walk up tenements mid-city
took to the highway as if there
avenues had migrated into boulevards
into four lanes with surely a crossing light
to break the monotony of cars
she brazened her way half a mile
to the mall road exit
the constant breeze of exhaust
fanning her skirts
no worse than dodging jitney cabs in the ghetto
she claimed ignoring my cautions
my mother like me had trouble
thinking of herself as elderly
what had to be done she did
until one day she fell on the gravel shoulder
and rolled into a ditch where no one
stopped to help as she dragged herself
along gathering spilled goods
the evening's meal morning's repast
all that my father blind at home awaited
I think of her now as I haul the bounty
of my own life out of traffic
the will to move on greater than age

Blood Lines

family ritual
>the breeze cools the dining room table
>where gossip boils in ceramic bowls

writing exercise:
>your memory is on fire
>how many blues songs can you save

wish bones
>mothers pulled both ends
>the best for children either way

what's left unsaid
>pictures carried in the eyes of the dead
>life by word of mouth

cat's cradles
>Jackson taught the sweetest
>fingers always escaped

survival exercise:
>your memory is underwater try saving
>a glass doll your birth father gifted

geography exercise
>Kingshighway and Natural Bridge
>boulevards bordering what you knew

exercise in cooking
>Bisquik, neck bones, chicken backs
>big black pot with wire coil handle

books to save
>Shakespeare hampered by your birth
>oh Fraility thy name is daughter

piece work
>what the ladies called cleaning white folks houses
>a steady job and pennies in a mason jar

your favorite dessert
        evaporated milk and banana slices
        frozen in the ice cube tray

combs and brushes
        a fine toothed rakes snarls
        into half forgotten memories

winnowing
        emulsion of glue and paper
        lives you know redacted

detritus
        is that you standing in the shadow
        while Mama smiles at the camera

chalk it up
        transmigrations transformations iterations
        sold and gone run away and gone grown up gone

neither girl nor woman
        the wind blew strong summer evenings
        so noisy eavesdropping

photographs to keep
        your mother in a chic hat
        chin cradled in a fox fur collar

look again
        your father in uniform a brand new mustache
        who's that baby all toothy grinning

now run along home
        bed already unmade under worn quilts
        in the mirror your mother's face startles you

ACKNOWLEDGMENTS

These poems have appeared in somewhat different forms in the following publications:

"A Sounding in the Woods," "The Family Album," and "Twilight Sleep" in *Connotation Press: An Online Artifact*; "Double Dutch" in *River Styx*; "The Tongue" in *Fightin' Words*; "For the Want of a Shoe" in *december*; "The Hanged Man," "Badlands," and "Immersion" in *Black Renaissance Noir*; "Immutable Geography" in *terrain.org*; "The Weight of Silence," "Top Kick," and "Rough Trade" in *Arts Today* 1.10; "Missouri Blues" and "Did I Know You Back Then" in *Poet Lore*; "Lessons in Deportment" and "Learning to Love Bessie Smith" in *poemmemoirstory*; "Throwing Stones at the All White Pool," in *The Golden Shovel Anthology: Honoring the Continuing Legacy and Influence of Gwendolyn Brooks*; and "Gandy Dancer," "Sepia Women," and "The Fire Inside" in *Konch Magazine*.

Many thanks to Cece Durante Bloum for her generosity in allowing me to use lines from Jimmy Durante's song "Did You Ever Have the Feeling?"

My gratitude to the Estate of Charles Alston and to National Museum of African American History and Culture for granting permission to use Alston's *Walking* (1958; oil on canvas, 48 × 64 in.; © Charles Alston Estate Collection of National Museum of African American History and Culture, gift of Sydney Smith Gordon, TR2007-4) on the cover of this book.

Special thanks to Lou Oma Durand, my resident muse who inspired me to re-imagine this tapestry of stories, and to Valerie Trueblood for her generosity of time and careful reading of numerous drafts.

And especially to my daughter, Vanessa, for daringly rescuing lost photographs.

List of people in photographs on Part One page: (*top row from left*) Uncle Brother (Perry Lee Jr.); Mama (my grandmother Anna Belle) and her eldest daughter, Claudia; and Aunt Fannie; (*second Row from left*) Aunt Jessie; Aunt Fannie; Papa (my grandfather Perry Lee); Ruth (my mother); and Uncle Brother; Son (on Mama's side of the family); (*bottom row from left*) Aunt Dora Emma (on Papa's side of the family); Purcia Purcell (my birth father); and Papa (circa the St. Louis Worlds Fair)

List of people in photographs on Part Two page: (*top row from left*) Uncle Phillip, my mother, Aunt Jennie, and Aunt Claudia; Uncle Brother and Aunt Jennie; (*second row from left*) Aunt Jennie, Aunt Ethel (my grandmother's sister), and Aunt Claudia; my mother; (*bottom row from left*) my mother, Uncle Brother, and Aunt Jennie; my mother and father (Jesse Dalton)